FOR MINE EYES HAVE SEEN THY
SALVATION

ABOUT THE PAINTINGS

These paintings were created to bring

life to the story of Christ. They provide

a glimpse into the happenings of His

ministry, a snapshot of what it might

have been like for the Saviour to walk

this earth, and a visual picture to

illustrate the written word of the Bible.

FOR MINE EYES HAVE SEEN THY
SALVATION

WRITTEN BY ROY LESSIN   PAINTINGS BY BRIAN JEKEL

DEDICATED TO CHRISTIANS
WHO WILL AND HAVE PUT
THEIR TRUST IN JESUS CHRIST.

FOR MINE EYES HAVE SEEN THY
SALVATION

© 2003 *The Master Peace Collection,*®
a brand of DaySpring® Cards.

Written by *Roy Lessin*
Paintings by *Brian Jekel*

Art Direction: Todd Knowlton

Book Design: Moe Studio

Printed in China

ISBN: 1-58061-734-4

CONTENTS

A WORD FROM THE AUTHOR

It is easy to think of the word "salvation" as an experience that comes into our lives when we receive Jesus Christ. The salvation that is found in the Bible has a much deeper and broader meaning; it is not just an experience that happens in a given moment but is a life-changing reality that continues throughout our time on earth and into eternity.

While holding the baby Jesus in his arms, Simeon spoke these words, "Mine eyes have seen Thy Salvation" (Luke 2:30). It is clear that his use of the word "salvation" referred to a person–not an experience. Salvation is Jesus Christ. Salvation abides in the heart of each person who receives Jesus Christ. This means that we can never have the experience of salvation without the Person of Salvation. In its fullest sense, salvation is all that Jesus is *to* us and *for* us. Salvation is our deliverance, freedom, aid, victory, prosperity, wholeness, health, and total well-being.

As you read this book, it is my prayer that your heart will celebrate, with an even deeper joy, the salvation that is yours in Jesus Christ. If you have never received God's glorious gift of Salvation, a prayer is included at the back of the book that will help guide you in asking Jesus Christ to be your Salvation. For those who have known the Lord but find themselves in a time of weariness or heaviness on their journey, may the Lord restore to you the joy of your Salvation (Psalm 51:12).

Roy Lessin

THE ANNUNCIATION

THE ANNUNCIATION

"AND IN THE SIXTH MONTH THE ANGEL GABRIEL WAS SENT FROM GOD UNTO A CITY OF GALILEE, NAMED NAZARETH, TO A VIRGIN ESPOUSED TO A MAN WHOSE NAME WAS JOSEPH, OF THE HOUSE OF DAVID; AND THE VIRGIN'S NAME WAS MARY. AND THE ANGEL CAME IN UNTO HER, AND SAID, 'HAIL, THOU THAT ART HIGHLY FAVOURED, THE LORD IS WITH THEE: BLESSED ART THOU AMONG WOMEN.' AND WHEN SHE SAW HIM, SHE WAS TROUBLED AT HIS SAYING, AND CAST IN HER MIND WHAT MANNER OF SALUTATION THIS SHOULD BE. AND THE ANGEL SAID UNTO HER, 'FEAR NOT, MARY: FOR THOU HAST FOUND FAVOUR WITH GOD. AND, BEHOLD, THOU SHALT CONCEIVE IN THY WOMB, AND BRING FORTH A SON, AND SHALT CALL HIS NAME JESUS. HE SHALL BE GREAT, AND SHALL BE CALLED THE SON OF THE HIGHEST: AND THE LORD GOD SHALL GIVE UNTO HIM THE THRONE OF HIS FATHER DAVID: AND HE SHALL REIGN OVER THE HOUSE OF JACOB FOR EVER; AND OF HIS KINGDOM THERE SHALL BE NO END.' "

" 'I, EVEN I, AM THE LORD; AND BESIDE ME THERE IS NO SAVIOUR.' "

"...WE SHOULD LIVE SOBERLY, RIGHTEOUSLY, AND GODLY, IN THIS PRESENT WORLD; LOOKING FOR THAT BLESSED HOPE, AND THE GLORIOUS APPEARING OF THE GREAT GOD AND OUR SAVIOUR JESUS CHRIST."

LUKE 1:26-33 • ISAIAH 43:11 • TITUS 2:12, 13
K J V

THE ANNUNCIATION

WHEN MARY WAS ENGAGED to Joseph, she experienced a day so extraordinary that it would take her a lifetime to ponder the depths of its meaning. During that day, she was visited by an angel, was told that she would conceive a child even though she was a virgin, and discovered that the child she would carry would be the long-awaited Messiah.

Mary didn't need to search a book of baby names to find one she liked. She received the name through the angel that God sent to her. When we give names to our children, we don't always think about the meaning of the name. Many babies today are given names just because they sound different or unusual, not because they have a certain meaning. Yet whenever God names a baby in the Bible, the name always has great significance and meaning. Mary's child would be called Jesus, a name that meant He would be the Saviour. The title "Saviour" was one that belonged to God alone. Therefore, Jesus' name meant that He was not only man, but that He was God come in the flesh.

In one major city in the United States, there is a church with a large neon sign at the top of the building. Travelers can see the sign from miles around. The sign reads, "Jesus Saves." Sometimes people who have seen this sign shining brightly over the city have asked, "Jesus saves from what?" The answer is a simple one. Jesus saves from sin. Jesus didn't come to leave us hopelessly bound in our sins. Jesus came to cleanse us from sin, forgive us, and to deliver us from its power in our lives. Jesus truly is a WONDERFUL Saviour.

God Knew Our Greatest Need

If our greatest need had been information, God would have sent us an educator.
If our greatest need had been technology, God would have sent us a scientist.
If our greatest need had been money, God would have sent us an economist.
If our greatest need had been pleasure, God would have sent us an entertainer.
But our greatest need was forgiveness, so God sent us a Saviour.

THANK YOU,

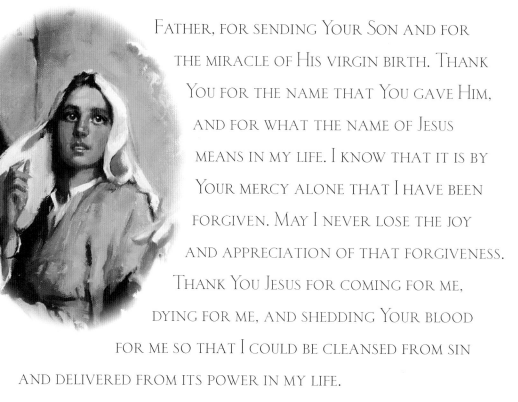

FATHER, FOR SENDING YOUR SON AND FOR the miracle of His virgin birth. THANK YOU for the name that YOU gave HIM, and for what the name of JESUS means in my life. I know that it is by YOUR mercy alone that I have been forgiven. MAY I never lose the joy and appreciation of that forgiveness. Thank You Jesus for coming for me, dying for me, and shedding Your blood for me so that I could be cleansed from sin and delivered from its power in my life.

SIMEON'S BLESSING

SIMEON'S BLESSING

"AND, BEHOLD, THERE WAS A MAN IN JERUSALEM, WHOSE NAME WAS SIMEON; AND THE SAME MAN WAS JUST AND DEVOUT, WAITING FOR THE CONSOLATION OF ISRAEL: AND THE HOLY GHOST WAS UPON HIM. AND IT WAS REVEALED UNTO HIM BY THE HOLY GHOST, THAT HE SHOULD NOT SEE DEATH, BEFORE HE HAD SEEN THE LORD'S CHRIST. AND HE CAME BY THE SPIRIT INTO THE TEMPLE: AND WHEN THE PARENTS BROUGHT IN THE CHILD JESUS, TO DO FOR HIM AFTER THE CUSTOM OF THE LAW, THEN TOOK HE HIM UP IN HIS ARMS, AND BLESSED GOD, AND SAID, 'LORD, NOW LETTEST THOU THY SERVANT DEPART IN PEACE, ACCORDING TO THY WORD: FOR MINE EYES HAVE SEEN THY SALVATION, WHICH THOU HAST PREPARED BEFORE THE FACE OF ALL PEOPLE; A LIGHT TO LIGHTEN THE GENTILES, AND THE GLORY OF THY PEOPLE ISRAEL.' "

LUKE 2:25-32
K J V

SIMEON'S BLESSING

THE ACCOUNT OF SIMEON holding the baby Jesus in his arms moves our hearts and touches us at the deepest level of our emotions. It is an account like none other. Simeon was not a rich man, an influential man, or a famous man—but he was a devout man. To him, the things of God really mattered. One day the Spirit of God revealed an incredible thing to Simeon: before God's time on earth for him was completed, he would see the Messiah. The One for whom Israel had hoped and waited would be seen by his eyes and held in his hands. He would actually witness and experience what Abraham, Moses, David, Isaiah, and Jeremiah could only speak about in prophetic wonder.

What a moment it was when Simeon gathered the baby in his arms, gazed upon His face, and lifted the child toward the heavens in worship and awe. In that moment, the light of the world was seen upon Simeon's countenance, the Incarnate Word of God was gripped within his fingers, and the blessings of God's wonders were upon his lips. When Simeon saw Jesus, it was the crowning moment of his life. His response to God for giving him this moment of pure joy was, "Take me home Lord. I'm ready. If I lived another hundred years on earth, no other moment could exceed the beauty of this moment in my heart."

The words of blessing that flowed from Simeon that day only add to the wonder of what God had revealed to him. He said that he saw not only the Christ child, but also God's salvation. That utterance moved the meaning of salvation away from the temple and from ritual to a person. Simeon knew that Jesus didn't *have* the light of hope and truth, but that He *was* the light of hope and truth. Simeon also knew that Jesus didn't *carry* the glory of Israel, but that He *was* the glory of Israel. Whatever God desired to bring to His people, He would bring through His salvation. Whatever God desired to say to His people, He would say through His salvation. Whatever God desired to be to His people, He would be through His salvation.

LORD,

THANK YOU FOR YOUR FAITHFULNESS TO

SIMEON, AND FOR FULFILLING IN HIS LIFE

EXACTLY WHAT YOU HAD PROMISED HIM.

I KNOW THAT YOU ARE ALSO FAITHFUL IN

MY LIFE, AND THAT YOU WILL FULFILL ALL

THAT YOU HAVE PROMISED ME. HOW

BLESSED I AM TO BE BLESSED BY YOU.

THANK YOU FOR THE LIGHT THAT YOU

HAVE SHED UPON MY PATHWAY, FOR THE

PEACE THAT YOU PLACED IN MY HEART, AND

FOR THE GLORY THAT MY EYES OF FAITH HAVE

SEEN IN YOUR SON, JESUS CHRIST. I REJOICE TODAY IN

KNOWING THAT YOU ARE MY SALVATION—NOTHING COULD

BE BETTER THAN THAT!

JESUS IN THE TEMPLE

JESUS IN THE TEMPLE

"AND THE CHILD GREW, and waxed strong in spirit, filled with wisdom: and the grace of God was upon Him. Now His parents went to Jerusalem every year at the feast of the Passover. And when He was twelve years old, they went up to Jerusalem after the custom of the feast. And when they had fulfilled the days, as they returned, the Child Jesus tarried behind in Jerusalem; and Joseph and His mother knew not of it. But they, supposing Him to have been in the company, went a day's journey; and they sought Him among their kinsfolk and acquaintance. And when they found Him not, they turned back again to Jerusalem, seeking Him. And it came to pass, that after three days they found Him in the temple, sitting in the midst of the doctors, both hearing them, and asking them questions. And all that heard Him were astonished at His understanding and answers. And when they saw Him, they were amazed: and His mother said unto Him, 'Son, why hast Thou thus dealt with us? Behold, Thy father and I have sought Thee sorrowing.' And He said unto them, 'How is it that ye sought Me? Wist ye not that I must be about My Father's business?' And they understood not the saying which He spake unto them. And He went down with them, and came to Nazareth, and was subject unto them: but His mother kept all these sayings in her heart. And Jesus increased in wisdom and stature, and in favour with God and man."

Luke 2:40-52
K J V

JESUS IN THE TEMPLE

THERE ARE SO MANY things about the incarnation of Jesus Christ (God becoming man) that leave us in amazement and wonder. Jesus was completely God and completely man. He was the God/Man. Throughout His life and ministry, the focus of Scripture is sometimes placed upon His humanity and sometimes upon His deity. In Jesus' visit to the temple, we see Him as a young man who is about to enter His teenage years. When Joseph and Mary find Him, Jesus is seated in the midst of teachers. Think of it—the One who is the Wisdom of God asked questions; the One who is the Lord of all sat at the feet of others; the One who is the Word of God grew in wisdom.

In a sense, this one brief glimpse that the Scriptures give us of Jesus' young life is a "preview of coming attractions." It is like seeing a movie trailer of God's feature presentation that would be released for the public's viewing in seventeen years. In this preview, we see a scene that reveals Jesus' heart. We see, in some detail, what motivated Him and what His character was like. It is no wonder that those who observed Him in the temple and spoke with Him were astounded.

The responses of Jesus toward those in the temple and to Joseph and Mary are the responses that God desires to see in every human heart—a priority to be "about God's business," a longing after His Word, and a hunger to grow in wisdom. He desires that we have Jesus' humility to listen and learn, His boldness to speak forth the heart and mind of God, and His meekness that submits to the authority of others.

FATHER,

You are good and Your ways are beyond comprehension. I bow in awesome wonder at the birth, the growth, and the development of Your Son as He matured from a child into a man. All that I see in Him is what I desire You to accomplish in me. I give You my heart; fill me. I give You my mind; instruct me. I give You my will; lead me. I give You my voice; speak through me. I give You my hands; use me. This day may I be about Your business.

THE BAPTISM OF CHRIST

THE BAPTISM OF CHRIST

"THE NEXT DAY John seeth Jesus coming unto him, and saith, 'Behold the Lamb of God, which taketh away the sin of the world....' And John bare record, saying, 'I saw the Spirit descending from heaven like a dove, and it abode upon Him. And I knew Him not: but He that sent me to baptize with water, the same said unto me, "Upon whom thou shalt see the Spirit descending, and remaining on Him, the same is He which baptizeth with the Holy Ghost." And I saw, and bare record that this is the Son of God.' "

" 'God anointed Jesus of Nazareth with the Holy Ghost and with power: who went about doing good, and healing all that were oppressed of the devil; for God was with Him.' "

" 'Ye shall receive power, after that the Holy Ghost is come upon you: and ye shall be witnesses unto Me both in Jerusalem, and in all Judaea, and in Samaria, and unto the uttermost part of the earth.' "

John 1:29, 32-34 • Acts 10:38 • Acts 1:8
K J V

THE BAPTISM OF JESUS

NO ONE WAS MORE dependent upon the
Holy Spirit and His ministry than Jesus Christ. Jesus was conceived
by the Holy Spirit, and the Spirit indwelt Him throughout His entire life.
As Jesus grew into adulthood, He was taught by the Holy Spirit.
At the waters of baptism, He was anointed by the Holy Spirit
for public ministry. During His ministry, He was led by the Holy Spirit.

Jesus loved the Holy Spirit and honored the Spirit's ministry in His life.
He knew that without such ministry, He could not do the will of the
Father. There was great delight in Jesus' words when He told the disciples
that when He went away, He would send the Holy Spirit to them.

Soon after the Holy Spirit came upon Jesus at His baptism, He stood
in the Synagogue and spoke these words, "The Spirit of the Lord is upon
Me, because He hath anointed Me to preach the gospel to the poor;
He hath sent Me to heal the brokenhearted, to preach deliverance to
the captives, and recovering of sight to the blind, to set at liberty them
that are bruised" (Luke 4:18 KJV). It is an amazing thing to realize that
Jesus did all His mighty works and wonders, not only because
He was God, but because the Holy Spirit anointed Him.

We who love and serve Jesus Christ are also totally dependent
upon the presence, ministry, and anointing of the Holy Spirit in
our lives. Jesus has promised to not only send the Holy Spirit into
our lives to indwell us, but He has also promised to send the
Holy Spirit upon us to empower us to serve Him and be
His witnesses in the world.

LORD,

thank You for the gift and ministry of the Holy Spirit in my life. Thank You that it is through Him that I can live the life that You have called me to live, and to serve You effectively. I ask You now to fill me and empower me with the Holy Spirit just as You have promised. May all that I do be in His strength and for Your glory. Amen.

WOMAN AT THE WELL

WOMAN AT THE WELL

"THEN COMETH HE TO a city of Samaria...
Now Jacob's well was there. Jesus therefore, being wearied
with His journey, sat thus on the well: and it was about the
sixth hour. There cometh a woman of Samaria to draw
water: Jesus saith unto her, 'Give Me to drink.' ...Then saith
the woman of Samaria unto Him, 'How is it that Thou, being
a Jew, askest drink of me, which am a woman of Samaria?'
For the Jews have no dealings with the Samaritans. Jesus
answered and said unto her, 'If thou knewest the gift of God,
and who it is that saith to thee, "Give Me to drink;" thou
wouldest have asked of Him, and He would have given thee
living water.' The woman saith unto Him, 'Sir, Thou hast
nothing to draw with, and the well is deep: from whence then
hast Thou that living water?...' Jesus answered and said unto
her, 'Whosoever drinketh of this water shall thirst again:
but whosoever drinketh of the water that I shall give him
shall never thirst; but the water that I shall give him shall
be in him a well of water springing up into everlasting life.'
The woman saith unto Him, 'Sir, give me this water, that
I thirst not, neither come hither to draw.' "

"...'If any man thirst, let him come unto Me, and drink. He that
believeth on Me, as the Scripture hath said, out of his belly
shall flow rivers of living water.' "

John 4:5-15 • John 7:37, 38
K J V

WOMAN AT THE WELL

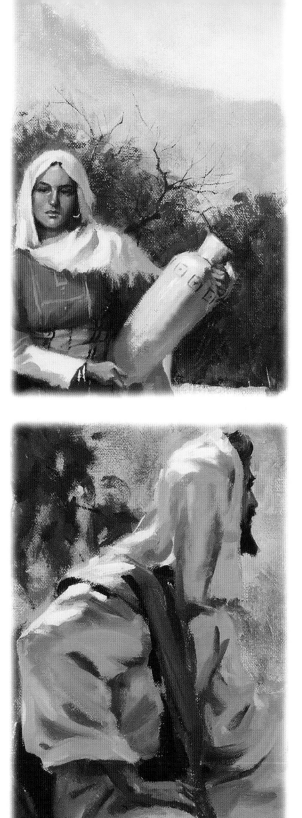

WHEN JESUS FACED a need of His own, it was often an opportunity to also minister to the needs of others. When He arrived in Samaria, weary from His journey, His need was for water from a well, but the woman that He met at the well had a need for water from the Spirit. Jesus found this opportunity for ministry because He was willing to go to a city that others avoided, and He was willing to talk to a woman that others had ignored. Jesus often showed up in unexpected places, at unexpected times, with unexpected responses, and produced unexpected results. Jesus once showed up at a gravesite, not to bury the dead, but to raise the dead; He once showed up during a storm at sea, not to ride out the storm, but to calm it; He once showed up at a chief tax collector's house, not to condemn the man, but to redeem him.

Through His words to the woman at the well, we find that Jesus always points the way to life. When He finds darkness, He presents Light; when He finds misunderstanding, He speaks Truth; when He finds thirst, He offers Living Water. Like the woman at the well, Jesus knows us like no one else can. He knows about every hurt, rejection, and disappointment we've experienced. In our need, He doesn't come to pat us on the back, but to lift us up. He doesn't come to give us positive thinking, but to give us joy. He doesn't come to offer us a list of steps, but to give us Himself.

The things in life that don't flow from His Spirit have no staying power. They last for a brief season and vanish away. What seems like living water soon turns to dryness, what seems like newness of life soon turns to disappointment, and what seems like satisfaction soon turns to discontent. Jesus' interests in us are much higher than temporary patch-up jobs or short-term solutions. He desires to give us, in abundance, the things that will last forever. He offered the woman at the well the kind of water that would totally satisfy her spiritual thirst. He offered her more than a pitcher-full of water; He offered her the well itself! It was an artesian well, not one that you had to pump. It was a well that would be—moment by moment, circumstance through circumstance, day after day—springing up into everlasting life.

JESUS,

THANK YOU FOR SEEKING ME OUT AND
COMING TO ME WITH SO MUCH COMPASSION
AND MERCY. THANK YOU FOR THE FLOW OF
YOUR SPIRIT IN MY LIFE. THANK YOU THAT
YOU HAVE PLACED WITHIN ME A WELL THAT
WILL NEVER RUN DRY. THANK YOU TODAY
FOR LIFE, FOR JOY, FOR GOODNESS, AND FOR
EVERYTHING THAT FLOWS OUT FROM YOUR
HEART TO TOUCH MINE. MAY YOUR LIVING
WATER TOUCH THE HEARTS OF OTHERS THROUGH
ME TODAY. LORD, LET YOUR WATERS FLOW!

WALKING ON THE WATER

WALKING ON THE WATER

"...JESUS CONSTRAINED HIS disciples to get into a ship, and to go before Him unto the other side, while He sent the multitudesaway. And when He had sent the multitudes away, He went up into a mountain apart to pray: and when the evening was come, He was there alone. But the ship was now in the midst of the sea, tossed with waves: for the wind was contrary. And in the fourth watch of the night Jesus went unto them, walking on the sea. And when the disciples saw Him walking on the sea, they were troubled, saying, 'It is a spirit;' and they cried out for fear. But straightway Jesus spake unto them, saying, 'Be of good cheer; it is I; be not afraid.' And Peter answered Him and said, 'Lord, if it be Thou, bid me come unto Thee on the water.' And He said, 'Come.' And when Peter was come down out of the ship, he walked on the water, to go to Jesus. But when he saw the wind boisterous, he was afraid; and beginning to sink, he cried, saying, 'Lord, save me.' And immediately Jesus stretched forth His hand, and caught him, and said unto him, 'O thou of little faith, wherefore didst thou doubt?' And when they were come into the ship, the wind ceased. Then they that were in the ship came and worshipped Him, saying, 'Of a truth Thou art the Son of God.' "

"But I am poor and needy: make haste unto me, O God: Thou art my help and my deliverer; O Lord, make no tarrying."

MATTHEW 14:22-33 • PSALM 70:5

K J V

Walking on the Water

JESUS IS THE PERFECT deliverer. A deliverer is someone who can carry us away to safety. Our deliverer knows the way of escape when we are trapped; He knows how to untie the knots if we are bound; He knows how to rescue us when we are over our heads in troubled waters. Before any difficulty reaches us, He has already worked out the solution to our deliverance.

As the account of the disciples' difficulty at sea begins to unfold, we discover some important insights into the Lord's deliverance in their lives. The first thing we see is that the difficulty came while the disciples were still within the Lord's will. The enemy can lie to us when we are facing difficulty by telling us that if we were in the Lord's will, we wouldn't be facing such difficulty. This lie, if believed, will make us feel condemned and can keep us from crying out to Jesus for deliverance.

The second thing we see is that Jesus was praying before the difficulty arrived. It is very important to our faith to realize that Jesus, our intercessor, covers our life with prayer. Regardless of the difficulty we face, we will never fully know all the things that we have been spared because Jesus prayed.

The third thing we see is that when the disciples cried out in fear, Jesus was immediately there. There is no delay in His response to our cries. When the disciples cried out, Jesus assured them of His presence. When Peter was sinking, Jesus didn't extend His hand and say, "Grab on!" Instead, Jesus reached out and took hold of Peter's hand. The Lord knows that in every crisis, if He didn't take hold of us, we would surely sink to the bottom.

The last thing we see is that Jesus is never overcome by the circumstance. When Jesus comes into a crisis in our lives, He takes over. He can speak to any storm and say, "You've howled enough—now be still."

JESUS,

THANK YOU THAT YOU ARE MY PERFECT
DELIVERER. THANK YOU THAT YOUR HAND
HAS TAKEN A HOLD OF MINE WITH THE GRIP
OF GRACE AND MERCY. WHERE WOULD I BE
WITHOUT YOU? THANK YOU THAT I CAN
CRY OUT TO YOU IN TIME OF TROUBLE,
AND THAT YOU DO NOT DELAY IN YOUR
RESPONSE TO ME. WHERE MY FAITH IS
SMALL, INCREASE IT; WHERE MY FAITH IS
WEAK, STRENGTHEN IT; WHERE MY FAITH IS
LIMITED, EXPAND IT. AMEN.

JESUS WITH THE CHILDREN

JESUS WITH THE CHILDREN

"AT THE SAME TIME CAME THE DISCIPLES
UNTO JESUS, SAYING, 'WHO IS THE GREATEST IN THE KINGDOM OF
HEAVEN?' AND JESUS CALLED A LITTLE CHILD UNTO HIM, AND SET HIM
IN THE MIDST OF THEM, AND SAID, 'VERILY I SAY UNTO YOU, EXCEPT YE
BE CONVERTED, AND BECOME AS LITTLE CHILDREN, YE SHALL NOT
ENTER INTO THE KINGDOM OF HEAVEN.' "

"AND THEY BROUGHT YOUNG CHILDREN TO HIM, THAT HE
SHOULD TOUCH THEM: AND HIS DISCIPLES REBUKED THOSE THAT
BROUGHT THEM. BUT WHEN JESUS SAW IT, HE WAS MUCH DISPLEASED,
AND SAID UNTO THEM, 'SUFFER THE LITTLE CHILDREN TO COME
UNTO ME, AND FORBID THEM NOT: FOR OF SUCH IS THE KINGDOM
OF GOD. VERILY I SAY UNTO YOU, WHOSOEVER SHALL NOT RECEIVE
THE KINGDOM OF GOD AS A LITTLE CHILD, HE SHALL NOT ENTER
THEREIN.' AND HE TOOK THEM UP IN HIS ARMS, PUT HIS HANDS
UPON THEM, AND BLESSED THEM."

"BECAUSE YE ARE SONS, GOD HATH SENT FORTH THE SPIRIT
OF HIS SON INTO YOUR HEARTS...."

MATTHEW 18:1-3 • MARK 10:13-16 • GALATIANS 4:6
K J V

JESUS WITH THE CHILDREN

WHEN JESUS SPOKE to people about the Kingdom of God, He didn't point them to the mind of a proud scholar, but to the heart of a little child. Jesus made it clear that the Kingdom of God belonged to the humble, not to the self-righteous; to the dependent, not to the self-sufficient; to the hungry, not to the self-satisfied. In the heart of a little child we find curiosity, spontaneity, simplicity, openness, and most of all, complete and uncomplicated trust. When Jesus was in the presence of little children, He didn't stick out His arms and push them away, but He opened His arms and blessed them.

There is no better way to live than to know that your life is in Jesus' hands and that His blessing is upon you. Every trusting heart can be certain of these things today:

You never need to think of yourself as forsaken, because Jesus has called you His own.
You never need to think of yourself as alone, because Jesus is with you always.
You never need to think of yourself as rejected, because Jesus holds you in His arms.
You never need to think of yourself as defenseless, because Jesus is your protector.

You never need to think of yourself as inadequate, because Jesus is your provider.
You never need to think of yourself as useless, because Jesus has a purpose and plan for your life.
You never need to think of yourself as hopeless, because Jesus is your future.
You never need to think of yourself as defeated, because Jesus is your victory.

You never need to think of yourself as weak, because Jesus is your strength.
You never need to think of yourself as perplexed, because Jesus is your peace.
You never need to think of yourself as needy, because Jesus is your daily provider.
You never need to think of yourself as unappreciated, because Jesus is your everlasting reward.

JESUS,

I come to You with a trusting
heart. I need Your wisdom, teach me;
I need Your power, strengthen me;
I need Your direction, guide me;
I need Your health, quicken me;
I need Your peace, settle me;
I need Your blessing, cover me;
I need Your presence, walk with me;
I need Your love, fill me.

JESUS IN THE TEMPLE

JESUS IN THE TEMPLE

"JESUS KNOWING THAT the Father had given all things into His hands, and that He was come from God, and went to God; He riseth from supper, and laid aside His garments; and took a towel, and girded Himself. After that He poureth water into a bason, and began to wash the disciples' feet, and to wipe them with the towel wherewith He was girded. Then cometh He to Simon Peter: and Peter saith unto Him, 'Lord, dost Thou wash my feet?' Jesus answered and said unto him, 'What I do thou knowest not now; but thou shalt know hereafter.' Peter saith unto Him, 'Thou shalt never wash my feet.' Jesus answered him, 'If I wash thee not, thou hast no part with Me.'...So after He had washed their feet, and had taken His garments, and was set down again, He said unto them, 'Know ye what I have done to you? Ye call me "Master" and "Lord:" and ye say well; for so I am. If I then, your Lord and Master, have washed your feet; ye also ought to wash one another's feet. For I have given you an example, that ye should do as I have done to you.'"

" 'But he that is greatest among you
shall be your servant.' "

JOHN 13:3-15 • MATTHEW 23:11
K J V

CHRIST'S EXAMPLE

PEOPLE GET UNCOMFORTABLE around Jesus because He doesn't fit into the way they see things, plan things, and do things. With our natural minds, we can never really understand what Jesus is all about. When we place Him next to our human plumb lines, He appears to be on a slant to the way we function; when we put a level next to Him, He looks out of balance to the way we react; when we put a ruler on Him, He doesn't seem to measure up to the way we go about our business. Jesus' entire life has been an enigma to many. The natural mind asks, "How could a prince be born outside a palace, a teacher have no degree, a king have no army, a ruler have no place to lay his head, and a miracle worker be unable to come down from a cross?"

When we see the way that Jesus responded to His disciples as they gathered for the Passover, we are once again amazed at His behavior. Even Peter could not fully grasp it. Peter saw himself as the follower and Jesus as the Master. "Why," he questioned, "would my Master take the place of a slave and wash my feet?" Peter had been with Jesus for more than three years but still had many things to learn. As Jesus washed the disciples' feet, He was doing far more than teaching them a lesson in humility; He was demonstrating to them what was at the heart of the Kingdom of God. The message of the Kingdom is that every follower of Jesus Christ carries a towel and washbasin with him into every circumstance and relationship in life. Jesus showed us that the Kingdom of God is "upside down" to the way the world operates.

In the Kingdom of God…
a person is lifted up by humbling himself, not by exalting himself in the eyes of others; strength is found through weakness, not by being confident in your own abilities; fullness comes by becoming empty, not by running after pleasure; life is gained by losing it, not by looking out for "number one"; riches come by giving them away, not by storing them up; greatness comes by becoming a servant, not by seeking power and celebrity.

LORD,

THANK YOU FOR YOUR KINGDOM AND FOR TURNING MY LIFE "RIGHT-SIDE-UP." THANK YOU FOR THE TOWEL AND WASHBASIN THAT YOU HAVE PLACED IN MY HANDS TO SERVE OTHERS. WORK IN ME THE HEART OF A SERVANT AS I RESPOND TO OTHERS IN THE WAYS OF A SERVANT. CONTINUE TO OPEN THE EYES OF MY UNDERSTANDING TO SEE THINGS THROUGH YOUR EYES AND TO RESPOND AS YOU WOULD RESPOND. TEACH ME MORE ABOUT YOUR KINGDOM AND WHAT IT MEANS TO ESTEEM OTHERS, TO HONOR THOSE TO WHOM HONOR IS DUE, AND TO LAY DOWN MY LIFE AS A LIVING SACRIFICE, HOLY AND ACCEPTABLE TO YOU.

GETHSEMANE'S PRAYER

"THEN COMETH JESUS WITH THEM UNTO A PLACE CALLED GETHSEMANE, AND SAITH UNTO THE DISCIPLES, 'SIT YE HERE, WHILE I GO AND PRAY YONDER.' AND HE TOOK WITH HIM PETER AND THE TWO SONS OF ZEBEDEE, AND BEGAN TO BE SORROWFUL AND VERY HEAVY. THEN SAITH HE UNTO THEM, 'MY SOUL IS EXCEEDING SORROWFUL, EVEN UNTO DEATH: TARRY YE HERE, AND WATCH WITH ME.' AND HE WENT A LITTLE FARTHER, AND FELL ON HIS FACE, AND PRAYED, SAYING, 'O MY FATHER, IF IT BE POSSIBLE, LET THIS CUP PASS FROM ME: NEVERTHELESS NOT AS I WILL, BUT AS THOU WILT.' AND HE COMETH UNTO THE DISCIPLES, AND FINDETH THEM ASLEEP, AND SAITH UNTO PETER, 'WHAT, COULD YE NOT WATCH WITH ME ONE HOUR? WATCH AND PRAY, THAT YE ENTER NOT INTO TEMPTATION: THE SPIRIT INDEED IS WILLING, BUT THE FLESH IS WEAK.' HE WENT AWAY AGAIN THE SECOND TIME, AND PRAYED, SAYING, 'O MY FATHER, IF THIS CUP MAY NOT PASS AWAY FROM ME, EXCEPT I DRINK IT, THY WILL BE DONE.'"

MATTHEW 26:36-42
K J V

GETHSEMANE'S PRAYER

THE FIRST MAN, ADAM, began his life in the perfect center of God's will. The will of God was a glorious thing for Adam. When Adam saw what God's will meant for him, his heart could say, "Yes, let me in. Let me be a part of it; let me embrace all it means. I do it with great delight and celebration!" Adam lived in the midst of a lush, beautiful garden filled with every type of fruit-bearing tree and budding flower. There were rivers around him and sunshine over his head. Birds and friendly animals were everywhere, and God gave Adam a wife who would be his daily companion and friend. God's sweet presence was in the garden, and Adam communed with Him in the cool of each day.

Thousands of years later, there was another garden. Into this garden came the Son of Man. He too entered a garden in the perfect will of God, but it is here that the similarities end. The Son of Man entered this garden—not in the brightness of sunshine—but in the darkness of night. This wasn't a garden of celebration, but a garden of distress and deep sorrow. This wasn't a garden of songbirds and laughter, but a garden of weeping and travail of the soul. This wasn't a garden of warmth and caring companionship, but a garden of solitude and the outpouring of agonizing prayer. This wasn't a garden of flowing waters and soothing streams, but a garden where the cup of suffering that the Father had poured had to be fully taken.

During Jesus' hour in the garden of Gethsemane, His prayer reveals the greatest difference of all between this garden and the Garden of Eden. In the Garden of Eden, we find that even though Adam lived in a perfect world, He made a selfish choice. When Adam was faced with temptation and Satan's lies, his heart said, "God, not Your will, but mine be done." In the garden of Gethsemane, as Jesus faced temptation and Satan's greatest onslaught, Jesus responded with these words, "Father, not My will, but Yours be done." Through Adam's sinful response came sin and the judgment of death. Through Jesus' surrender and willing response came forgiveness and everlasting life.

JESUS,

THANK YOU FOR ALL YOU HAVE DONE

TO REDEEM ME AND MAKE ME YOUR OWN.

THANK YOU THAT WHEN YOU FACED THE

TEMPTATION OF SIN, YOU DIDN'T YIELD

TO IT; WHEN YOU FACED THE REJECTION

OF MEN, YOU DIDN'T RUN FROM IT; WHEN

YOU FACED THE ONSLAUGHT OF SATAN,

YOU DIDN'T FLEE FROM IT; WHEN YOU

FACED THE CUP OF SUFFERING, YOU DIDN'T

TURN FROM IT. BRING MY HEART TO THE

PLACE OF SAYING, "YOUR WILL BE DONE"

IN EVERY ASPECT OF MY LIFE.

JESUS BEFORE PILATE

JESUS BEFORE PILATE

"THEN PILATE ENTERED INTO THE JUDGMENT HALL AGAIN, AND CALLED JESUS, AND SAID UNTO HIM, 'ART THOU THE KING OF THE JEWS?' JESUS ANSWERED HIM, 'SAYEST THOU THIS THING OF THYSELF, OR DID OTHERS TELL IT THEE OF ME?' PILATE ANSWERED, 'AM I A JEW? THINE OWN NATION AND THE CHIEF PRIESTS HAVE DELIVERED THEE UNTO ME: WHAT HAST THOU DONE?' JESUS ANSWERED, 'MY KINGDOM IS NOT OF THIS WORLD: IF MY KINGDOM WERE OF THIS WORLD, THEN WOULD MY SERVANTS FIGHT, THAT I SHOULD NOT BE DELIVERED TO THE JEWS: BUT NOW IS MY KINGDOM NOT FROM HENCE.' PILATE THEREFORE SAID UNTO HIM, 'ART THOU A KING THEN?' JESUS ANSWERED, 'THOU SAYEST THAT I AM A KING. TO THIS END WAS I BORN, AND FOR THIS CAUSE CAME I INTO THE WORLD, THAT I SHOULD BEAR WITNESS UNTO THE TRUTH. EVERY ONE THAT IS OF THE TRUTH HEARETH MY VOICE.' PILATE SAITH UNTO HIM, 'WHAT IS TRUTH?' AND WHEN HE HAD SAID THIS, HE WENT OUT AGAIN UNTO THE JEWS, AND SAITH UNTO THEM, 'I FIND IN HIM NO FAULT AT ALL.' "

"FIGHT THE GOOD FIGHT OF FAITH, LAY HOLD ON ETERNAL LIFE, WHEREUNTO THOU ART ALSO CALLED, AND HAST PROFESSED A GOOD PROFESSION BEFORE MANY WITNESSES. I GIVE THEE CHARGE IN THE SIGHT OF GOD, WHO QUICKENETH ALL THINGS, AND BEFORE CHRIST JESUS, WHO BEFORE PONTIUS PILATE WITNESSED A GOOD CONFESSION; THAT THOU KEEP THIS COMMANDMENT WITHOUT SPOT, UNREBUKEABLE, UNTIL THE APPEARING OF OUR LORD JESUS CHRIST."

JOHN 18:33-38 • I TIMOTHY 6:12-14

K J V

JESUS BEFORE PILATE

WHEN PEOPLE ASKED Jesus questions, He always gave them the answers their hearts needed to hear. Pilate was no exception. If Pilate's heart had truly been seeking to know who Jesus was, he would have found Him to be not only the King of the Jews but also his own personal King. But Pilate was seeking facts, not truth.

Jesus made two statements in response to Pilate's questions that were beyond the man's understanding. When Pilate asked Jesus, "What hast Thou done?" Jesus answered, "My kingdom is not of this world." Pilate was looking for an answer that would give some kingly credentials with which to validate Jesus' kingship, but Jesus' kingdom couldn't be found on a map. Jesus did not have a treasury that could be seized, property that could be destroyed, or an army that could be captured. He conquered people with goodness, ruled them with righteousness, and governed them with love. Who could combat a kingdom like that?

Jesus' other statement came when Pilate asked Him, "Art Thou a king then?" and Jesus replied, "To this end was I born, and for this cause came I into the world, that I should bear witness unto the truth." Pilate wanted solid evidence that Jesus might use in His defense. But Jesus didn't need defending. The hearing before Pilate was not about Jesus defending His innocence with facts so that He could be released; it was about Jesus bearing witness to the truth so that He could go to the cross. Based upon the facts, Jesus should have been released, for there was no evidence against Him. But based upon the truth, Jesus went to the cross because that was why the Father had sent Him. When Pilate asked, "What is truth?" he did so because he had rejected the truth. The truth stood before Pilate's throne, but Pilate didn't recognize Him; the truth looked in Pilate's eyes, but Pilate couldn't see Him; the truth spoke to Pilate's ears, but Pilate couldn't hear Him. Only those who want the truth, love the truth, and are willing to be changed by the truth will know the One who is the Truth.

JESUS,

I receive You as the King of my life.
Thank You that You reign in my heart.
May my attitudes be under the scepter
of Your righteousness, may my choices
be governed by the rule of Your will,
and may my motives be in conformity
with the Kingdom of Your love. Make
me a faithful witness of the truth to
all those that You bring into my life.

ROAD TO THE CROSS

ROAD TO THE CROSS

"THEN SAITH PILATE UNTO HIM, 'Speakest Thou not unto me? Knowest Thou not that I have power to crucify Thee, and have power to release Thee?' Jesus answered, 'Thou couldest have no power at all against Me, except it were given thee from above: therefore he that delivered Me unto thee hath the greater sin.' And from thenceforth Pilate sought to release Him: but the Jews cried out, saying, 'If thou let this Man go, thou art not Caesar's friend: whosoever maketh himself a king speaketh against Caesar.' When Pilate therefore heard that saying, he brought Jesus forth, and sat down in the judgment seat...And it was the preparation of the Passover, and about the sixth hour: and he saith unto the Jews, 'Behold your King!' But they cried out, 'Away with Him, away with Him, crucify Him.' Pilate saith unto them, 'Shall I crucify your King?' The chief priests answered, 'We have no king but Caesar.' Then delivered he Him therefore unto them to be crucified. And they took Jesus, and led Him away. And He bearing His cross went forth into a place called the place of a skull, which is called in the Hebrew Golgotha."

JOHN 19:10-17
K J V

ROAD TO THE CROSS

JESUS WALKED ON MANY ROADS during His brief time on earth. The roads He walked led Him through valleys and over hilltops, through crowed city streets and quiet villages, and to people's homes and festive celebrations—but the road that led Him to the place of crucifixion was the one He was born to travel. The Father watched from heaven as His Son, beaten and bruised, staggered under the weight of the cross on His way to a place called Golgotha. Jesus knew that this road was the only way His love could find a place in our hearts. If God would have set a roadblock on this road and said to His Son, "Road closed," we would never have found our way to Him.

It is Jesus' journey with the cross and His crucifixion upon Golgotha's hill that opens our understanding to the meaning of love at its deepest level. Salvation is our free gift that cost Jesus everything—His brokenness means that we can be made whole; His sorrow means that we can have fullness of joy; His rejection means that we can be accepted; His pain means that we can be healed; His death means that we can have life everlasting.

A man once had an old vase that he kept in a cardboard box in his attic. One spring day the man was cleaning out his attic in preparation for his wife's upcoming garage sale. The old vase wound up on a table with a sticker price of $2.00. All the early birds passed over the vase. Around noon, a man who was an antique dealer spotted the vase. "I don't think you want to sell this for $2.00," the dealer told the owner. "I'll take less," the owner replied. "You don't understand," said the dealer. "This vase is very rare and highly valuable. I could sell it in my shop for $2,500." The owners were shocked! Once they discovered the true value of the vase, they removed it from the table, carefully cleaned it, and placed it in a prominent place in their home.

The devil has convinced so many people that they are as worthless as the dusty old vase in the attic—and they have reinforced the lie by the way they live. Each of us needs to stop and remember the cross—it is here that we will discover our true value. It is here that we discover the price God was willing to pay for us, and how much we are worth to Him.

LORD,

I am overwhelmed with Your love for me. Where would I be without You? Thank You for loving me so much that You willingly left Your home in heaven and came to earth to suffer and die for me. I am overjoyed with the good news that I have been forgiven, cleansed, and set free from my sins so that I may know You and enjoy You forever. May the way I live and the choices I make be a way of honoring the value that You have placed upon life. Amen.

MARY AT THE TOMB

MARY AT THE TOMB

"MARY STOOD WITHOUT AT THE SEPULCHRE WEEPING: AND AS SHE WEPT, SHE STOOPED DOWN, AND LOOKED INTO THE SEPULCHRE, AND SEETH TWO ANGELS IN WHITE SITTING, THE ONE AT THE HEAD, AND THE OTHER AT THE FEET, WHERE THE BODY OF JESUS HAD LAIN. AND THEY SAY UNTO HER, 'WOMAN, WHY WEEPEST THOU?' SHE SAITH UNTO THEM, 'BECAUSE THEY HAVE TAKEN AWAY MY LORD, AND I KNOW NOT WHERE THEY HAVE LAID HIM.' AND WHEN SHE HAD THUS SAID, SHE TURNED HERSELF BACK, AND SAW JESUS STANDING, AND KNEW NOT THAT IT WAS JESUS. JESUS SAITH UNTO HER, 'WOMAN, WHY WEEPEST THOU? WHOM SEEKEST THOU?' SHE, SUPPOSING HIM TO BE THE GARDENER, SAITH UNTO HIM, 'SIR, IF THOU HAVE BORNE HIM HENCE, TELL ME WHERE THOU HAST LAID HIM, AND I WILL TAKE HIM AWAY.' JESUS SAITH UNTO HER, 'MARY.' SHE TURNED HERSELF, AND SAITH UNTO HIM, 'RABBONI;' WHICH IS TO SAY, 'MASTER.' JESUS SAITH UNTO HER, 'TOUCH ME NOT; FOR I AM NOT YET ASCENDED TO MY FATHER: BUT GO TO MY BRETHREN, AND SAY UNTO THEM, "I ASCEND UNTO MY FATHER, AND YOUR FATHER; AND TO MY GOD, AND YOUR GOD." ' MARY MAGDALENE CAME AND TOLD THE DISCIPLES THAT SHE HAD SEEN THE LORD, AND THAT HE HAD SPOKEN THESE THINGS UNTO HER."

"I MAY KNOW HIM, AND THE POWER OF HIS RESURRECTION...."

JOHN 20:11-18 • PHILIPPIANS 3:10
K J V

MARY AT THE TOMB

THE LAST WORDS JESUS spoke before His death on the cross were, "It is finished." The debt of our sin had been paid in full. Yet even though the work of redemption was finished, Jesus was not finished. Three days later, Jesus was raised from the dead by the power of God. It was the greatest triumph of all. Jesus had not only conquered sin, but He had conquered death! It is the complete work of Jesus Christ—His birth, His life, His death, and His bodily resurrection—that makes salvation sure for all who believe. Truly, the Gospel of Jesus Christ is the power of God unto salvation.

The Ten Most Powerful Things In The Universe That Can Revolutionize Your Life:

1. *The Power of the Blood of Jesus* – nothing else can cleanse you from sin.
(I JOHN 1:7)

2. *The Power of the Gospel* – nothing else can save your soul.
(ROMANS 1:16)

3. *The Power of the Cross* – nothing else can deliver you from yourself.
(ROMANS 6:6)

4. *The Power of the Word* – nothing else can bring you transforming truth.
(JOHN 17:17)

5. *The Power of God* – nothing else can keep you from evil.
(MATTHEW 6:13)

6. *The Power of the Holy Spirit* – nothing else can make you like Jesus.
(II CORINTHIANS 3:18)

7. *The Power of the Resurrection* – nothing else can give you eternal hope.
(1 PETER 1:3)

8. *The Power of Prayer* – nothing else can move the hand of God.
(MATTHEW 21:22)

9. *The Power of Grace* – nothing else can make you completely sufficient.
(II CORINTHIANS 9:8)

10. *The Power of Faith* – nothing else can keep you till the end.
(I PETER 1:5)

© Roy Lessin 2003

LORD JESUS,

IN EVERY WORD, IN EVERY ACTION,

IN EVERY CIRCUMSTANCE, IN EVERY

WAY...BE MIGHTY IN ME BY THE

POWER OF YOUR HOLY SPIRIT!

AMEN.

"RESTORE UNTO ME

———————————————————

THE JOY OF THY SALVATION;

———————————————————

AND UPHOLD ME

———————————————————

WITH THY FREE SPIRIT."

PSALM 51:12 KJV

Jesus,

I thank You that You are the

Saviour. I know that You not only *give*

the gift of Salvation, but that You *are* the gift

of Salvation. Thank You for leaving heaven, coming

to earth, dying on the cross for my sins, and rising from

the dead. I ask You to forgive me. I turn away from my

sins and all that has kept me from You. I open my heart

to You and receive You now by faith as my Lord and

Saviour. Jesus, come into my life and take over.

Thank You for Your mercy and love and

for being my Salvation today.

Amen.